Like the Singing Coming off the Drums

Like the Singing Coming off the Drums

~ *Love Poems* ~

Sonia Sanchez

BEACON PRESS

BOSTON

BEACON PRESS
25 Beacon Street
Boston, Massachusetts 02108-2892
http://www.beacon.org

BEACON PRESS BOOKS
are published under the auspices of
the Unitarian Universalist Association of Congregations.

Grateful acknowledgment is made for the permission to reprint from the poem
"A Luta Continua" from *When the Clouds Clear* by Keorapetse Kgositsile.

03 02 01 00 99 98   8 7 6 5 4 3 2 1

Text design by Elizabeth Elsas
Composition by Wilsted & Taylor Publishing Services

LIBRARY OF CONGRESS CATALOGING-IN-PUBLICATION DATA
Sanchez, Sonia, 1935–
     Like the singing coming off the drums : love poems / Sonia Sanchez.
        p.   cm.
     ISBN 0-8070-6842-x
     1. Love poetry, American.   I. Title.
     PS3569.A468L5   1998
     811'.54—dc21   97-33326

to Afeni and Tupac Amaru Shakur

Sections

Naked in the Streets

DANCING

i dreamt i was tangoing with
you, you held me so close
we were like the singing coming off the drums.
you made me squeeze muscles
lean back on the sound
of corpuscles sliding in blood.
i heard my thighs singing.

HAIKU

you ask me to run
naked in the streets with you
i am holding your pulse.

SONG

i cannot stay home
on this sweet morning
i must run singing   laughing
through the streets of Philadelphia.
i don't need food or sleep or drink
on this wild scented day
i am bathing in the waves of your breath.

HAIKU

let every breast dance
a wild sculpture of rain
i raise my glass.

TANKA

i don't know the rules
anymore i don't know if
you say this or not.
i wake up in the nite
tasting you on my breath.

HAIKU

i count the morning
stars the air so sweet i turn
riverdark with sound.

HAIKU

i come from the same
place i am going to my
body speaks in tongues.

HAIKU

i have caught fire from
your mouth now you want me to
swallow the ocean.

HAIKU [*for you*]

love between us is
speech and breath. loving you is
a long river running.

POEM

mornings taking a
detour from love wide
assed life spilling starch.

HAIKU

i await your touch
come magnify our smell
make of us a long journey.

HAIKU

i turn westward in
shadows hoping my river
will cross yours in passing.

SONKU

i collect
wings what are
you bird or
animal?
something that
lights on trees
breasts pawnshops
i have seen
another
path to this
rendezvous.

BLUES HAIKU

when we say good-bye
i want yo tongue inside my
mouth dancing hello.

BLUES HAIKU

you too slippery
for me. can't hold you long or
hard. not enough nites.

TANKA

i thought about you
the pain of not having
you cruising my bones.
no morning saliva smiles this
frantic fugue about no you.

HAIKU

hunger comes on morning
sails. where twilight passes me
wide is the river.

SONKU

1.
i who have
never moved
from where i
was born could
tell you names
dates posit
memory
when you kid
napped my blood
i retired
into my sex.

2.
and i thought
mountains were
men but these
Makonde
Mountains breasts
whispering
spiraling
sound these wo
men mountains
long with curves

caress   dance
in a suite
of heavy thighs
sweet mountains
smelling me.

HAIKU

come windless invader
i am a carnival of
stars a poem of blood.

HAIKU

i am moving in
air amazon woman bare
foot thunderbound bells.

HAIKU

[on passing Toni Cade Bambara's house]

how are we here one
day gone the next how do we
run fall down to death?

HAIKU

[*for Bernice*]

now i move in the
blood of women who polish
pores a cappella.

HAIKU

i cry out for the
company of women de
liberate with blood.

HAIKU

what is done is done
what is not done is not done
let it go . . . like the wind.

BLUES HAIKU

what i need is traveling
minds talktouch kisses spittouch
you swimming upstream.

HAIKU

old man standing long
carrying your shanghai years
like an old rickshaw.

TANKA

men who watch in the
night see me coming and yell
the leper comes the
leper comes who will feed her
she without friend or lover.

HAIKU

it is i who have
awakened in nakedness
o cold the morning cock.

TANKA

this man has sucked too
many nipples been inside
too many holes grid
locked too many skins to
navigate a blackwomansail.

HAIKU

i am watersnake
crossing your long body
hear me turn in blood.

HAIKU

i am the ugly
duckling the second daughter
eyes shaking like leaves.

HAIKU

have you ever crossed
the ocean alone seen the
morning cough yellow?

HAIKU

mixed with day and sun
i crouched in the earth carry
you like a dark river.

BLUES [*for Deb*]

even though you came in december be my january man,
i say, even though you came in december be my january man,
but you know i'll take you any month i can.

woke up this morning, waiting for you to call
say, i woke up this morning waiting for you to call
started shaking in my bed, thought i was taking another fall.

fortune teller, fortune teller, what you forecast for me today,
fortune teller, fortune teller, what you forecast for me today,
cuz i ain't got no time to be messing with yo yesterday.

even though you came in december be my january man,
i say, even though you came in december be my january man,
but you know i'll take you any month i can
but you know i'll take you any month i can.

HAIKU

how fast is the wind
sailing? how fast did i go
to become slow?

BLUES HAIKU

let me be yo wil
derness let me be yo wind
blowing you all day.

BLUES HAIKU

am i yo philly
outpost? man when you sail in
to my house, you docked.

HAIKU

my womb is a dance
of leaves sweating swift winds
i laugh with guitars.

HAIKU [*for Joanne*]

sweet woman dancing
your morning sails i see
your riverbound legs.

POEM

1.
i am dreaming
i have spread my dreams out like wings.
i have selected today a dream
about flying and i take off
sailing on your blue smile.
for today it is enough.

2.
all this year
i have heard
my pores
opening.

3.
i have told
you my name
so there is
tomorrow.

4.
see me through
your own eyes
i am here.

5.
let us be one with
the earth expelling anger
spirit unbroken.

6.
we are
only
passing
through let
us touch.

7.
come again inside
me let us take another
turn at loving.

8.
i hear your smell
running across my threshold.
shall i hold your breath?

Shake Loose My Skin

SONKU [*for Nneka and Quincy*]

love comes with
bone and sea
eyes and rivers
hand of man
tongue of
woman love
trembles at
the edge of
my fingers.

HAIKU

c'mon man hold me
touch me before time love me
from behind your eyes.

TANKA

c'mon man ride me
beyond smiles teeth corpuscles
come into my bloodstream
abandon yourself to smell let
us be a call to prayer.

I gather up
each sound
you left behind
and stretch them
on our bed.
           each nite
I breathe you
and become high.

HAIKU

how still the morning sea
how still this morning skin
anointing the day.

SONKU

i feel your
mouth on my
thighs immac
ulate tongue.

SONKU

i hear the
sound of love
you unstring
like purple beads
over my breasts

HAIKU

i am who i am.
nothing hidden just black silk
above two knees.

HAIKU

in a season of
beautiful clowns betrayals
unapologetic.

HAIKU [*question from a young sister*]

1.
what's wrong with being
freaky on stage you a stone
freak in yo own skin.

2.
at least we up front
about this freakdom. at least
we let it all hang out.

Good morning, sex. How do you do?
Tell me how life's been treating you.
You say what? Sex is and sex ain't
sex wuz and sex wuzn't
sex should be and sex has been
on Times Square billboards
on television, in the movies,
in the lyrics dripping off pouting lips.
You say sex is in the drinks we drink
the laughs we laugh
the walk we walk
the smells we smell as we open
our eyes and legs and let the funk spread.
You say sex is dark basements
lights turned out, bodies turned on.
Sex is a breakfast table full of
leftover wine and smiles.
Sex is kinky & clean shaven
sex is straight & gay
sex is do it anyway.
Comes in twos and threes.
Comes on time. Late.
Sex is love. Unlove.

Comes with danger & beauty
Comes in clean and shadowy places.
Sex is life. Death. A gig.
Sometimes you need it in the
Morning. Afternoon. Evening.
Sometimes it satisfies; sometimes it don't
sometimes you feel it in yo' armpits
sometimes you feel it in the mind,
but ah, *ahhh*, when it comes
this sex, when it appears
buck naked or clothed,
when it comes Thelonious Monk–like jazzy,
when it comes hip hopping like the nite
ain't like no other nite; ya
know what time it is, what day
it is, what month it is, what year
it is. When it comes RIGHT, you
understand that sex is & sometimes it ain't
But when it is. . . .

BLUES HAIKU

i ain't yo momma
but i am this lil mama
who knows how to burn.

BLUES HAIKU [*for Joanne and Val*]

yall talkin all under
my clothes bout my love bizness
friends be doin that.

this is not a fire
sale but i am in heat
each time i see ya.

HAIKU

i am you loving
my own shadow watching
this noontime butterfly.

BLUES HAIKU

i wuz in Kansas
dorothy and toto wuzn't
a jacuzzi. sky. you.

HAIKU

i am looking for
you to banish all sermons
a fine hail of touch.

HAIKU [*for Nneka and Quentin*]

i listen to this blood
breathing roses in my veins.
i grow with laughter.

HAIKU

these waves boisterous like
Che's mountains smell of mania
howling in my veins.

HAIKU [*for Louis Massiah*]

your leonine eyes
squatting in Du Boisian blood.
violets and steel.

SONKU

what is love
you asked
i took you
inside be
hind my eyes
and saw me.

BLUES HAIKU

legs wrapped around you
camera. action. tightshot.
this is not a rerun.

BLUES HAIKU

is there a fo rent
sign on my butt? you got no
territorial rights here.

BLUES HAIKU

my face is a scarred
reminder of your easy
comings and goings.

HAIKU

derelict with eyes
i settle in a quiet
carnival of waves.

HAIKU

the i in you the
you in me colliding in
one drop of semen

HAIKU

i taste your sweet salt come
your face a revelation
of bedtime fairy tales.

HAIKU [*for Queen Mother Moore*]

they smell like rust
these truants shouting magic
obscure men in heat.

HAIKU

a tint on the tongue
an echo in the fingers
i dust off your cough.

HAIKU

my teeth can write your
name in hieroglyphics paint
your sound graffiti-like.

HAIKU

i have carved your face
on my tongue and i speak you
in my off-key voice.

SONKU

my eyes look
and i don't
see me i
turn around
to find you.

SONKU

when i die
i shall take
your smell
inside me.

HAIKU

i am a small piece
of yellow flesh taking shelter
like a leper.

BLUES HAIKU

his face like chiseled
china his eyes clotting
around rubber asses.

to be lifted in
smoke to be cast in iron
remembering the fire.

TANKA

woman without heat
blankets herself with eyes
avoiding the cock's walk.
a woman in seclusion
dreams of secreting milk.

HAIKU

it was nothing big
just no one to put suntan
lotion on my back.

the sea murmuring
dialect remember che
alive in my veins.

SONKU

what i want
from you can
you give? what
i give to
you do you
want? hey? hey?

HAIKU

i hear your breath
in the faraway room
breathing castanets.

HAIKU

i smell you on my
skin ravishing my veins
i see your sweat running.

HAIKU

[for Joe Barry]

when i imagine
you i recall a river
flowing with eyes.

HAIKU

red orange breasts sweet
as chocolate touch my lips
wild bones up for sale

HAIKU

and i am flesh burnt
red charcoal black gift wrapped in
philadelphia blood.

HAIKU

this poem is for me
who could not speak your death
still i laugh and spin

SHORT POEM

quite often without
you i am at a loss for
the day.

HAIKU 1   [*for Bill and Camille*]

but i am left with
flesh that hangs like yellow sails
hear my voice knocking.

HAIKU 2

my bones migrate in
red noise like pinched wings
they stream white ashes.

HAIKU

do you want ashes
where your hands used to be
other faces will come.

HAIKU

if i were an old
woman all my veins could hold
my laughter in check.

HAIKU

you are rock garden
austere in your loving
in exile from touch.

TANKA

to surround yourself with
arms that will not hold you
to dream yourself home
where the road is dust
and dissolves in purple.

SONKU

to worship
until i
become stone
to love
until i
become bone.

HAIKU

[for Bill and Camille]

my bones hang to
gether like pinched dragonflies
shake loose my skin.

In This Wet Season

HAIKU [*for Sophie and Val*]

in this wet season
of children raining hands
we catch birds in flight.

A POEM FOR ELLA FITZGERALD

when she came on the stage, this Ella
there were rumors of hurricanes and
over the rooftops of concert stages
the moon turned red in the sky,
it was Ella, Ella.
queen Ella had come
and words spilled out
leaving a trail of witnesses smiling
amen—amen—a woman—a woman.

she began
this three agèd woman
nightingales in her throat
and squads of horns came out
to greet her.

streams of violins and pianos
splashed their welcome
and our stained glass silences
our braided spaces
unraveled
opened up
said who's that coming?

who's that knocking at the door?
whose voice lingers on
that stage gone mad with
    perdido. perdido. perdido.
    i lost my heart in toledooooooo.

whose voice is climbing
up this morning chimney
smoking with life
carrying her basket of words
                a tisket a tasket
                my little yellow
                basket—i wrote a
                letter to my mom and
                on the way i dropped it—
                was it red . . . no no no no
                was it green . . . no no no no
                was it blue . . . no no no no
                just a little yellow

voice rescuing razor thin lyrics
from hopscotching dreams.

we first watched her navigating
an apollo stage amid high-stepping
yellow legs

we watched her watching us
shiny and pure woman
sugar and spice woman
her voice a nun's whisper
her voice pouring out
guitar thickened blues,
her voice a faraway horn
questioning the wind,
and she became Ella,
first lady of tongues
Ella cruising our veins
voice walking on water
crossed in prayer,
she became holy
a thousand sermons
concealed in her bones
as she raised them in a
symphonic shudder
carrying our sighs into
her bloodstream.

this voice, chasing the
morning waves,
this Ella-tonian voice soft
like four layers of lace.

when i die Ella
tell the whole joint
please, please, don't talk
about me when i'm gone . . . .

i remember waiting one nite for her appearance
audience impatient at the lateness
of musicians,
i remember it was april
and the flowers ran yellow
the sun downpoured yellow butterflies
and the day was yellow and silent
all of spring held us
in a single drop of blood.

when she appeared on stage
she became Nut arching over us
feet and hands placed on the stage
music flowing from her breasts
she swallowed the sun
sang confessions from the evening stars
made earth divulge her secrets
gave birth to skies in her song
remade the insistent air
and we became anointed found
inside her bop

bop bop dowa
bop bop doowaaa
bop bop dooooowaaaa

Lady. Lady. Lady.
be good. be good
to me.
          to you.   to us all
cuz we just some lonesome babes
in the woods
hey lady. sweetellalady
Lady. Lady. Lady. be gooooood
ELLA ELLA ELLALADY
          be good
                    gooooood
                              goooooood . . .

A SONG FOR SWEET HONEY
IN THE ROCK

see me through
your own eyes
i am here.

don't look for me
in poems
i'm not there.

don't look for me in
shadowy faces
i'm not there.

see me through
your own eyes
i am here.

once. when or with whom
i disappeared went
into hiding behind
my own skull
wasn't seen for a decade or two
wasn't seen for a decade or two.

now i am back
carrying my life in a small bag
now i am back
holding open my hands
holding open my hands.

see me through
your own smile
i am here.

see me through
your own smell
i am here.

see me through
your own eyes
i am here
i am here . . .

LOVE POEM   [*for Tupac*]

1.
we smell the
wounds hear the
red vowels
from your tongue.

the old ones
say we don't
die we are
just passing
through into
another space.

i say they
have tried to
cut out your
heart and eat
it slowly.

we stretch our
ears to hear
your blood young
warrior.

2.

where are your fathers?
i see your mothers gathering
around your wounds folding
your arms shutting your
eyes wrapping you in prayer.

where are the fathers?
zootsuited eyes dancing
their days away.
what have they taught you
about power and peace.

where are the fathers
strutting their furlined
intellect bowing their
faces in the crotch
of academia and corporations
burying their tongues
in lunchtime pink
and black pussies
where are the fathers to teach
beyond stayinschooluse
acondomstrikewhilethe

iron'shotkeephopealive.
where have the fathers buried their voices?

3.
whose gold is carrying you home?
whose wealth is walking you through
this urban terror? whose greed
left you shipwrecked with golden
eyes staring in sudden death?

4.
you were in
a place hot
at the edge
of our minds.
you were in
a new world
a country
pushing with
blk corpses
distinct with
paleness and
it swallowed
you whole.

5.
i will not
burp you up.
i hold you
close to my heart.

LOVE CONVERSATION

[*AIDS day* 1994 *in Philadelphia, for Essex Hemphill*]

How are you doin sistah?
  fine
how you doin girl?
  i said i was doin okay.
But how you really doing
  i said i'm okay, didn't i?
  Gotta go now. Have to get
  home to my daughter.
Sistah, Sistah, Sistah, i'm not
trying to interfere. But how
you makin out? Heard
you wuz sick
  i'm fine i said just
  fine didn't i just
  say i'm fine. I'm okay
  i'm standing here talkin
  to you ain't i?
I know but how you really
doing really feeling really
getting along. i want to help
heard you wuz real sick

allright. I'm hanging in
there standing up sitting down
spaced out scared talkin
silent laughing screaming
screaming screaming
legs hurt body hurt
eyes hurt chest hurt when
i cough all nite
don't sleep a lot
sweat all night long
body wrapped in wet sheets
that's how i am you know
and i call on my Gods
to help me through the nite
oya olukun oya olukun oya
sistah. I want ya to
know that i'm i'm i'm i'm
I ammmmmm here
and until i pass over
you will see me
walkin talkin lovin
prayin organizin bein
cuz i ammmmmmm
the universe knows that
i ammmmmmm
hiv positive but i ammmm

still. woman. lover. mother.
sistah. artist. organizer. activist.
woman
i say you will remember me
my life and my love
becuz i ammmmmmm a woman
soy mujer
mujer soy
i am.

FOR TUPAC AMARU SHAKUR

who goes there? who is this young man born lonely?
who walks there? who goes toward death
whistling through the water
without his chorus? without his posse? without his song?

it is autumn now
in me autumn grieves
in this carved gold of shifting faces
my eyes confess to the fatigue of living.

i ask: does the morning weep for the dead?
i ask: were the bullets conscious atoms entering his chest?
i ask: did you see the light anointing his life?

the day i heard the sound of your death, my brother
i walked outside in the park
we your mothers wanted to see you safely home.
i remembered the poems in your mother's eyes as she
panther-laced warred against the state;
the day you became dust again
we your mothers held up your face green with laughter
and i saw you a child again outside your mother's womb

picking up the harsh handbook of Black life;
the day you passed into our ancestral rivers,
we your mothers listened for your intoxicating voice:
and i heard you sing of tunes bent back in a
cold curse against black

       against black (get back)

       against black (get back)

we anoint your life
in this absence
we anoint our tongues
with your magic. your genius.
casual warrior of sound
rebelling against humiliation

    ayyee—ayyee—ayyee—

    i'm going to save these young niggaz

    because nobody else want to save them.

    nobody ever came to save me. . . .

your life is still warm
on my breath, brother Tupac
Amaru Shakur
and each morning as i
pray for our people
navigating around these

earth pornographers
and each morning when
i see the blue tint of
our Blackness in the
morning dawn
i will call out to you again:

where is that young man born lonely?
and the ancestors' voices will reply:
he is home tattooing his skin with
white butterflies.

and the ancestors will say:
he is traveling with the laughter of trees
his reptilian eyes opening between the blue spaces.

and the ancestors will say:
why do you send all the blessed ones home early?
and the ancestors will say:
you people. Black. lost in the memory of silence.
look up at your children
joined at the spine with death and life.
listen to their genius in a season of dry rain.
listen to them chasing life falling
down getting up in this
house of blue mourning birds.

listen.

    & he says: i ain't mad at ya

    & we say: so dont cha be mad at yo self

    & he says: me against the world

    & we say: all of us against the world

    & he says: keep yo head up

    & we say: yeah family keep yo head up every day

    & he says: dear mama, i love you

    & we say: dear all the mamas we love you too

    & he says: all eyez on me

    & we say: kai fi African (come here African)

                 all eyez on ya from the beginning of time

                          from the beginning of time

                 resist.

                 resist.

                 resist.

can you say it? resist. resist. resist.

can you say it? resist. resist. resist.

i say. can you do it? resist. resist. resist.

can you rub it into yo sockets? bones?

can you tattoo it on yo body?

so that you see. feel it strengthening you

as you cough blood before the world.

yeah. that's right. write it on your

forehead so you see yourselves as you walk past tomorrow

on your breasts so when
your babies suckle you, when your man woman
taste you they drink the milk of resistance. hee hee hee
take it inside you so when your lover. friend.
companion. enters you they are covered
with the juices, the sweet
cream of resistance. hee hee hee
make everyone who touches this mother lode
a lover of the idea of resistance.
can you say it? RESIST.
can you say it? RESIST.

til it's inside you and you resist
being an electronic nigger hating yo self & me
til you resist lying & gossiping & stealing &
killing each other on every saturday nite corner
til you resist having a baby cuz you want
something to love young sister. love yo self
til you resist being a shonuff stud fuckin
everything in sight, til you resist raping
yo sister, yo wife, somebody's grandmother.
til you resist recolonizing yo mind
mind mind mind mind

                              resist
                              resist
                              resist for Tupac

resist for you & me
reSIST RESIST RESIST
for Brother
Tupac
Amaru
Shakur

REMEMBERING AND HONORING
TONI CADE BAMBARA

how to respond to the genius
of our sister Toni Cade Bambara? How to
give praise to this brilliant. Hard. Sweet
talking Toni. Who knew everything.
Read everything. Saw everything?

I guess if we remember Willie Kgositsile's lines:

> *if you sing of workers you have praised her*
> *if you sing of brotherhood and sisterhood you*
> *have praised her*
> *if you sing of liberation you have praised her*
> *if you sing of peace you have praised her*
> *you have praised her without knowing*
> *her name*
> *her name is Spear of the Nation . . .*

I would also add:

> *her name is clustered on the hills*
> *for she has sipped at the edge of rivers*
> *her words have the scent of the earth*

and the genius of the stars
i have stored in my blood the
memory of your voice Toni linking continents
making us abandon Catholic minds.
You spread yourself rainbowlike
across seas
Your voice greeting foreign trees
Your voice stalking the evening stars.

And a generation of people began to question their silence. Their poverty. Their scarcity. Because you had asked the most important question we can ask ourselves:

What are we pretending not to know today? The premise as you said, my sister, being that colored people on the planet earth really know everything there is to know. And if one is not coming to grips with the knowledge, it must mean that one is either scared or pretending to be stupid.

You open your novel with the simple but profound question: Do we want to be well? And you said in an interview with Sister Zala Chandler that the answer tends to be "No! to be whole politically, psychically, spiritually, culturally, intellectually, aesthetically, physically, and economically whole—is of profound significance. It is significant because there is a correlative to this. There is a responsibility to self and to history that is developed once you are whole, once you are well, once you acknowledge your powers."

Amiri Baraka wrote that Jimmy Baldwin was God's black revolutionary mouth. So were you Toni. You made us laugh resistance laughter. You taught us how to improvise change shapes sometimes change skins. We learned that if we are to be, sometimes we must have been there already and have people wondering about us:

> *You asking about them colored folk?*
> *They were just here. Ain't they still there*
> *in place in Harlem, in Washington in*
> *Chicago? i just seen em a second ago*
> *they wuz dancing at the Palladium,*
> *picking cotton, having a picnic in*
> *the park drinking walking they*
> *sanctified walk talking they*
> *fast talk brushing the nightmare*
> *of America off they foreheads.*
> *Look there they be. That's them laughing*
> *that loud laugh over there. No that*
> *ain't them. They gone again like the wind.*
> *Oh. You asking for them people from*
> *forever ago time sifting time through*

hands, announcing they are here intend
to be here. Listen. Listen You can hear
them breathing breaths not even invented
yet. laughing their resistance. hee hee hee.
You got to find me to get me.

Get on board children.
This Bambara liberation train
of the spirit, soul. This Bambara
train doing what Audre Lorde said:
forever moving history beyond nightmare
into structures for the future . . .

Get on board this liberation train called Bambara. Cmon lil children. And Toni had many children. She taught us how to organize. Be. Their names are Aishah, Mungu, Karma, Kevin, D Knowledge, Ras, Nora, Louis, Tony, Morani. Gar.

This is how i lay down my Praise:

What seas came from her eyes!
What oceans connected us from her
Southern and Eastern bones!
What waterfall of Bambara words transformed
Our lives, our hands into miracle songs!

This is how i lay down my love:

We are not Robert Oppenheimer quoting
Indian literature: I have become death.
We are. Must be. Must quote,
i have become life
and oppose all killings, murderings,
rapings, invasions, executions,
imperialist actions.
i have become life
and i burn silver, red,
black with life for our children
for the universe for the sake
of being human.

What we know today is that this
earth cannot support murderers,
imperialists, rapists, racists, sexists,
homophobes. This earth cannot
support those who would invent
just for the sake of inventing
and become death.

We must all say i have
become life, look at me
i have become life

i move like the dawn with a tint of
blue in my hair
i say, i say
i have become life and
i walk a path that clears
away the debris of
pornographers.
i have become life, light,
life, light, life,
light and i move
with my eyes
My hands holding up life
for the world.
i have become life . . .

Aaayeee babo Aaaayeee babo

How do you praise a man who has traveled from Tulsa,
Oklahoma, the first American city that dropped a bomb
on an American community, to Harvard University?;

How do you see him walking always in his three-piece
black suit, giving us lessons in morality and life? Always
questioning the "morality" of the country/state/world
that has enslaved and continues to enslave all of its
citizens racially, and culturally, always questioning a
country that remains silent while people stain the earth
with their separate poverty, death, homelessness. Always
questioning a country that denies the sanctity, the
holiness of children, people, rivers, sky, trees, earth?;

I would say you look less at his credentials but more at
the living work. The actions of a man destined to walk a
preacher's walk. A philosopher's walk. A twenty-first-
century man walk;

I would say you look at the father in him. The husband in
him. The activist in him. The teacher in him. The lover

in him. The truth seeker in him. The James Brown dancer in him. The reformer in him. The defender of people in him. The intellectual in him;

I would say that at the end of the twentieth century, we will remember him as a man who was *present* and *bore witness* to the terrible beauty of this time and the possibility of reconciliation and redemption;

This man. Born into history. This humanist. This twenty-first-century traveler pulling us screaming against our will towards a future that will hold all of humankind in an embrace. He acknowledges us all. The poor. Blacks and whites. Asians and Native Americans. Jews and Muslims. Latinos and Africans. Gays and Lesbians;

For he has seen the leper in himself. In all of us. And he cries out against a policy of leperdom. No longer the yells from the cities.
>The leper comes. The leper comes.
>The leper comes. Who will feed
>her or him?

Thank you my Brother for patrolling our lives. Thank you for walking among the flowers and the columns.

Thank you for magnifying our souls and making of us
humans a long journey.

    Aaaayeee babo

    Aaaayeee babo

    Aaaayeee babo for Cornel West

               Cornel West

               Cornel West . . .

Aaayeee babo means Praise God.

132

you tell the stars
don't be jealous of her light
you tell the ocean,
you call out to Olukun,
to bring her always to
safe harbor,
for she is a holy one
this woman twirling
her emerald lariat
you tell the night
to move gently
into morning so she's
not startled,
you tell the morning
to ease her into a water
fall of dreams
for she is a holy one
restringing her words
from city to city
so that we live and
breathe and smile and
breathe and love and
breath her . . .
this Gwensister called life.